ASIA
UNPACKED

THE ULTIMATE HOW TO TRAVEL GUIDE

MARK CALDWELL
Founder of EziAsiaTravel

Travel.
Make memories.
Have adventures.
Because I guarantee that when
you're 85 and, on your death bed you
won't think about that flashy car you
bought, or the 20 pairs of designer
shoes you owned.
But you will think about that time
you got lost in your favourite city.
The nights spent falling in love
under the stars and all the beautiful
people you met along the way. You'll
think of the moments that made you
feel truly alive. And at the very
end, those memories will be the only
valuable possessions you own.
-EKP-

TABLE OF CONTENTS

Batu Caves, Kuala Lumpur, Malaysia

WELCOME TO ASIA UNPACKED

I have travelled many times to Asia, have learnt so much. but at the same time had my share of issues. I have purchased many travel books; all gave me much-needed information and pinpointed locations that I subsequently visited. On reflection, I found that I did not find any publication that gave me all the hints and tips that would save me from falling into the traps commonly experienced by novice travellers, especially those new to Asia. All the publications I was exposed to, showed me where to travel, where to stay and amazing places to visit. Nowhere, did I find information on how to travel. Whilst in travel limbo due to covid, I felt it was time (and I had the time) to fill this gap.

Travelling by bus, car, train and by plane, criss-crossing Asia, I have experienced the pros and cons of each mode of transport. I have grown to love some places and avoid others. I do recognise that it is all a matter of taste and personal choice. Some people go for the culture, some for the relaxed lifestyle, others for the nightlife. Whatever keeps bringing you back, you will find the beautiful nature of the people, the amazing food, awe-inspiring views coupled with the value for money fuelling your desire to keep going back year after year.

Many friends and colleagues have contacted me before going on their odyssey. They have asked me for advice, tips, and recommendations. I have always been happy to do this and have passed on contacts and recommendations for hotels and tours to suit their needs. It is common to be nervous and apprehensive about what you will experience in Asia. People are mainly concerned about what they can eat, whether they can drink the water, how to find the best place to stay, and how to cope in such a foreign environment to their normal lifestyle. I did my best to reassure them, but also to make them aware of ways in which to make their holiday less stressful.

It is important to recognise that scams and unforeseen issues happen in every country in the world. I have heard stories from friends who have been pickpocketed in Paris, others robbed in Spain and one friend recounts a horrific story of a physical attack in Florida. Nowhere in the world is fully free from issues, highlighting the need for preparation before embarking on any new adventure.

The idea of being a travel consultant was born from the urging of others to pass on the knowledge born from trial and error. I have travelled with friends and family members to Asia, passing on the many tips gathered along the coconut tree-lined pathways. The concept of EziAsiaTravel and subsequently ASIA UNPACKED was born as a way of passing on my love of the region and allowing others to share my experiences. I am confident that I can save you and your travel companions from making my inexperienced mistakes and save you from spending too much money where lower-cost options are available. I also believe not only new travellers will benefit from this book. Even I'm still learning about new places and new experiences from fellow travellers.

As I reside in Brisbane, Australia, I give examples of how to travel to Asia from airports close to home. In the first chapter, we explore the choices between low-cost and full-fare airlines, if you are reading this book elsewhere in Australia, or outside of Australia there are many travel apps available, giving you all the flying and pricing options from your closest departure point.

I am positive that when you read this book, you will be armed with valuable travel tips. You will feel more confident about travelling to Asia. Although no one is supremely confident crossing a road in Vietnam during peak hour traffic, with motorbikes coming towards you in multiple directions, it is possible, trust me. At the end of your holiday, you will be a travel pro, showing others how to cross the roads without fear (well, maybe a little fear, but you will not show it).

I have quoted prices in the following pages concerning airfares and accommodation and many other costings. All these are pre-covid examples and in Australian currency unless stated otherwise. I do believe that prices will be similar, once travel begins in large numbers. At the resumption of open travel, prices may be discounted to attract travellers to return in numbers, so check with travel apps and guides to confirm pricing options.

Ha long Bay, Vietnam

BOOKING A FLIGHT

DESTINATION AND ARRIVAL

It is time to book your flight. Firstly, determine which airport is the most advantageous arrival point. You may even have a choice of departure airports close to homebase.

If you are travelling to Asia from the east coast of Australia, namely, Brisbane, Sydney, or Melbourne, you have choices of more than one airport close to these cities. Firstly, determine where to first disembark in Asia. Common airports to consider, include Singapore, Bangkok, or Kuala Lumpur. These are the main hubs and have many costing options. Depending on where you are flying from, other options may be available.

Choices should be made considering the best options for ongoing travel plans. Each hub has differing options when travelling to your next destination. Always remember that you are on holiday and want to spend the least time as possible waiting in Airport lounges. Pre-trip research will avoid long stopovers and trying to sleep on uncomfortable plastic chairs. If you are arriving at the optimal hub, it will ensure a shorter transfer and an earlier arrival at your next destination.

My strategy is to use online flight apps. They will allow you to access the best options, departure and arrival times and any stopovers, airline choices and costings. With this information, go directly to the webpage of your airline of choice and book the flights on their site. Prices are generally similar. Some travel apps give you the choice to book and pay on unknown sites, but these can be unsafe, charge extra fees, and may affect insurance and refund chances. Travel agents make little margin from flights and will generally steer you toward full-fare options to increase income sources.

FULL FARE VS LOW-COST AIRLINES

Departing from Australia, you have the choice of purchasing full-fare seats with airlines including, Singapore Airlines, Malaysian Airlines and Thai Airways to mention a few, or you can fly at lower costs on airlines such as Scoot Air or AirAsia. Most of the low-cost airlines are owned by larger parent companies, Singapore Airlines own Scoot, Nok Air and Tiger. Malaysian Airlines own AirAsia or at the very least, they are major shareholders. These affiliations ensure the highest standard servicing and maintenance, you can rest assured that you are in safe hands.

Depending on your departure point around the world (pre-covid), most major airports are serviced by numerous cost options. Many online flight comparison sites are available to advise you as to your costs, length of flight and arrival options. I have a choice of departing from Brisbane or Gold Coast Airport. Scoot Airlines only travel from the Gold Coast to Singapore whilst AirAsia, both travel from Gold Coast to Kuala Lumpur and from Brisbane to Bangkok, hopefully these routes will return when flights return.

Depending on your location, you will need to research the options available to you. Once you have worked out your best departure airport, you will need to choose between available full fare, budget, or low-cost airlines. Cost is an important consideration. Pre-covid the basic cost was around $420 to $500 return on Scoot Airlines, from the Gold Coast to Singapore. This fare did not include checked-in luggage, meals, entertainment, or seat allocation. These extra options can be easily purchased before departure. Flights from Gold Coast departed around 9am and arrived in Singapore at approximately 3pm local time. I pre-purchased a meal and drink for around $10. Scoot allows ten kilos of cabin luggage in their overhead compartments. Be aware that Air Asia allow only seven kilos carry-on. This information is vital to allow you to decide if you need to purchase checked-in luggage before departure. Later chapters will show how to pack, what to pack, and how to travel with only carry-on luggage. If you want extra luggage, for a cost of around $30 or $50 you can purchase checked-in luggage. Prices are similar for AirAsia to Kuala Lumpur or Air Asia to Bangkok. Regarding full-service airlines, before the pandemic, a return flight to Singapore, flying Singapore Airlines (a full fare airline) from Brisbane, would cost around $800 to $1000 return, including all the in-flight options. Your choice is determined by your budget. Flight cost comparison online apps will give you your local costings.

Check prior to booking low-cost or full fare flights, whether the booking conditions allow refunds, change of timing of flights and name changes on your preferred flights. In some conditions your travel insurance will cover you. In the case that you need to make a change, full fare tickets can allow extra options. Changes on low-cost airlines are possible but will attract extra charges.

SEAT ALLOCATION

Unless you have special needs, the daylight timing and duration of flights to Singapore, Bangkok, and Kuala Lumpur from Australia, mean seat allocation is not necessary. If you are travelling from other parts of the world where an overnight flight both ways is the norm, seat allocation both ways will be something to consider as a pre-purchase option. The return flight from Asia to Australia normally departs close to midnight and arrives in Australia in the early morning, so seat allocation on the return leg can be especially important to allow for as much sleep as possible, in as much comfort as possible. Seat allocation starts at around $40.

With regards to onboard entertainment, if you booked a low-cost flight, simply load music, movies, and TV shows from streaming services onto your phone or device with personal headphones allowing you to listen during the flight without disturbing other passengers. On the return night flight, with regards to ordering a meal, as you arrive back early, breakfast on return to Australia is the best option. If returning to other parts of the world check flight duration and any stopovers to determine needed meal arrangements.

FLIGHT TRANSFERS

From Singapore, Bangkok, and Kuala Lumpur you can travel to most places directly in Asia on local airlines for under $100 (sometimes as low as $20) to most airports in Malaysia, Thailand, Cambodia, Laos, and Vietnam. Myanmar, at the time of writing, was experiencing civil unrest and maybe best to avoid, however, this could change in the future. If you are travelling from Australia's east coast, low-cost airlines should arrive late in the afternoon leaving you plenty of time to book a connecting flight to another destination on the same day. You can always book a stopover at your arrival point, stay a few days and travel after a few days' rest. If travelling from places other than Australia, I would recommend a few days rest before moving to your next destination.

FLYING IN ASIA

When travelling from country to country in Asia, the distances are commonly low (usually only an hour to an hour and a half at the most), therefore, low-cost airlines are a good option. Airlines like AirAsia, Tiger Airlines and Jetstar Asia, fly many times per day to popular destinations. It is recommended to arrange flights, if possible, to arrive mid-afternoon. Your hotel accommodation does not normally allow entry to your room until around two in the afternoon. You can wake at a leisurely hour, have breakfast, maybe fit in some sightseeing or a swim in the pool, before checking out and going to the airport. If arriving early is unavoidable most hotels are happy to hold your luggage while you do some sightseeing before your room's availability.

Airlines on occasions run specials for members. There are many advantages to joining. Scoot, in Australia, on tuesday mornings, offers a special member price. Check out local deals closer to home to make great saving. Booking flights internally in Asia can be confusing, online airline websites will give you all your options. It can be easier to work in reverse. Googling the desired airport will show the airlines that service that arrival point. It will also list direct flights into that airport. I use the app Flight Connections; this app will highlight the direct routes into any given airport. With this information, you can design your internal framework to minimise stopovers and delays when travelling.

PAPERWORK AND TICKETING.

These days there is no need to print out tickets, although I tend to print out my Itineraries. I can go over it to make sure I have not made any errors. Very importantly, when booking flights, use the name of the person exactly matching the name on their passport, if someone's passport says their first name is RAYMOND and you book a ticket using RAY instead of RAYMOND, you will encounter problems boarding that flight. It is likely you will eventually get on the plane, but it will cause problems at check-in. Ensure the name on your passport is an exact match with the ticket name, also ensure the date of birth, the passport number and issue and expiry dates match exactly.

BOOKING ACCOMMODATION

FRAMEWORK

When you are booking an overseas holiday your first task is to develop a framework for the holiday. What does that mean? In the last chapter, we learnt how to book flights, from your departure point to your arrival point. Then we discussed internal flights during your holiday. After you had booked your flights, added other modes of transport between destinations, you have your framework. Your accommodation holiday plans need to fit inside the transport framework. Accommodation cannot be booked until you know when you are arriving, how long you are staying and when you are departing. Now it's time to book your accommodation.

BOOKING ROOMS

Along with booking flights, budget is a factor when it comes to accommodation. Prices in Asia are much cheaper on average than accommodation prices in Australia, the US and Europe. Prices quoted are usually room costs (not per person costs) and you can find accommodation for as low as $5 a night if you are prepared to stay in low budget hotel rooms or hostels. I have seen hostels in Hanoi charging $5USD a night which included free breakfast and free beer. It is also good to remember that you are on holiday and unless you are on a shoestring budget, then it is okay to have a little luxury. There is no need to go for five-star accommodation unless you are happy to pay top dollar. I have stayed at some amazing three-star hotels in Asia that will have you coming back for more.

Singapore, Hong Kong, and Japan are an exception as accommodation is expensive by Asian standards and on par with western prices.

On my first trip to Asia, I booked according to location and price, I pre-booked twenty-eight nights of accommodation over six different cities, for no more than $30 a night for two people. These bookings also included a free buffet breakfast for two. After booking in at my first hotel in Kuala Lumpur, we found the room adequate, but no refrigerator and no pool in my pre-booked hotels. We could have paid extra and moved to an upgraded room just to get a refrigerator but declined. We did stay in the room for an additional four nights as the rooms were comfortable, and the location was perfect. We quickly realised that I could have made better choices.

Hostel in Old Quarter in Hanoi, look around and you can get great deals

BOOKING GUIDELINES

I now have a few personal guidelines when booking accommodation.

Location is number one. Book close to attractions, cafes, and transport hubs.

Secondly, and very importantly, it must have air conditioning, I also look for ceiling fans in combination with air conditioning (a personal choice) as the air conditioning can make the room too cool during the night, you may not have access to the temperate controls to change the airflow and temperature. As the temperature drops during the night, a fan is enough to ensure a comfortable night sleep. Night-time comfort is, of course, a personal choice. I will let you sort this one out based on your needs.

Thirdly, a hotel with a pool. It is normally extremely hot in Asia and cooling off in a swimming pool is a great solution.

Fourthly, ensure you have included breakfast in your booking package.

Finally, the option of free cancellation before arrival.

On my first trip, I used my free cancellation option once we identified the shortcomings of our original booking plan. We were able to change every booking online for the rest of the holiday. It did cost a little extra, about $20 a night. Once we had established guidelines, we were able to identify the accommodation that suited our needs.

REVIEWS

When I visit a new location, I research hotel booking sites like Booking.com and Trivago, to name a few, getting prices, facilities, and availability of rooms. I also view the maps provided to see the proximity to local attractions. It is important to read the reviews of travellers who have stayed at the property. These reviews are incredibly valuable as they will tell you information not included in the hotel's self-written story.

I discovered on a previous trip a nightclub close to booked accommodation. This nightclub was open until early morning and according to the reviews, very noisy. If you are someone who does not want to be in that nightclub maybe accommodation further away is for you. Reviews have also highlighted issues, such as construction going on near a property, where work may continue extremely late into the evening and on weekends as there are limited noise abatement laws in place in many countries. I have, when researching reviews, identified issues such as pool maintenance and subsequent pool closures during my planned stay as well.

BEST PRICES

Cost is important. A saving option to put in place, after you're booked (with free cancellation of course) can be to set up a price watch on your preferred booking site, for similar rooms, on the same dates, in the same hotel. On receiving an alert from the booking site, of a price change on similar rooms, in the same hotel, on the same days, it is a simple process to book the discounted rooms on the same nights in the same hotel. Remember, now you have two bookings, use the free cancellation option. Cancel the original higher priced booking.

Another savings option is to email the hotel direct. The hotel pays a fee to the booking service, ask them for a better price or maybe an upgrade if you book directly with them, instead of the booking service. Of course, once the discounted booking is confirmed directly to the hotel, cancel your original booking. It is a win-win: the hotel makes more money, you pay less, or you get more for your money.

REQUESTS AND CHANGES

In many cases, you will get an email from the hotel after your booking, welcoming you to the property. They will offer you extra services like airport pickups, tours, and spa treatments. In the coming chapters, you will access advice on tours and extra services once you have arrived. If you are travelling as a family or part of a group, you can make requests to the hotel for adjoining rooms or rooms on the same floor. Other requests are possible but will be at the discretion of the hotel. It is another good reason to read the reviews. Previous guests will pass on advice on where in the hotel to stay, where to get the best views, information on preferred sides of the building, or best choice on which floor is best and why. You can even take advantage of lower-priced drinks or food during happy hours, but only if you are aware of your options. Depending on your flights you can also ask for early or late check-in or check-out. I will admit that I have, after arrival, been unhappy with my accommodation and checked out and found other more suitable accommodation. As I have previously stated, you are on holiday, and there is nothing worse than staying somewhere you are not happy. Due to low costs, changing for the last few days, to stay in a more suitable hotel does not break the budget.

FINE PRINT AND REFUNDS

It is vital to read everything in the room description and hotel policies before making a booking. You can discover fine print showing that they will take the full cost of the booking any time after you have made the booking. This will not affect your free cancellation, but your money has left your bank account. You will get it back, if you cancel, using free cancellation options, but it may not be instantaneous. It is best to book hotels that indicate that you pay at the site or nothing to pay until you arrive.

Read the room description very well. Some of the lowest cost rooms advertised, may not have windows or balconies. They may be internal rooms, still comfortable but can be a bit stifling and claustrophobic.

On arrival, the hotel will take a pre-approval of your credit card, depending on your card an amount will be set aside to guarantee that you have sufficient funds to pay your costs. After departure, this pre-approved transaction will be cancelled, and an extra transaction will be charged to your card. The original amount will be refunded to your card, but this may take a few days to appear, and your funds are available. Keep this in mind if you are close to your credit limits. The use of debit cards is available but will take funds from your account, for a few days until refunded. Talk to your bank before travel.

LUGGAGE AND PACKING

CHOICES

So, what do you take with you, when going overseas? It does not seem on the surface to have much importance (until you start packing). It is important to consider, as it affects your transport options and costs. You do not want to be carrying huge amounts of luggage with you, on the other hand, not having enough clothing or essential items when you arrive is also a problem. During my first trip to the region, my travelling companion and I each lugged twenty kilos of check-in luggage and carry-on bags each of approximately seven kilos for a month. In stark contrast, on my last trip, I only had a seven-kilo carry-on bag for the month.

What happened? What made me downsize my packed choices? There was a cost to consider, if you are making five or six flights during your journey it can add up to $300 extra to your travel costs. The time you are wasting also cannot be ignored, when arriving at an airport after clearing immigration and customs, those without luggage travel straight through to the taxi rank, or your waiting car. You have started your holiday.

WHAT DO YOU PACK FOR ASIA?

When choosing what to pack, consider that the temperatures rarely drop below 30°C in summer or winter: loose cool clothing is essential. I recommend for a male traveller, taking three or four pairs of shorts, similar numbers of shirts and underwear, flip flops or sandals, with minimal toiletries.

On departure, the type of toiletries and amounts you can

take on board is limited to cabin regulations. Check with your carrier, but commonly, only containers sized less than 110mls, no aerosol containers and no sharp objects are allowed in carry-on luggage. In most hotels, a range of free personal toiletry items are commonly provided, although, shampoo and conditioner can be a bit dodgy. If you need extra items a quick visit to a convenience store will allow you to buy what you need at low prices.

The cost of laundry is ridiculously low and is a cheaper option than lugging lots of clothes and paying luggage costs on airlines. Many shop front laundries will charge $1USD per kilogram. You will rarely pay more than $2USD per kilogram for washing. Drop off your washing as you need. The hotels also offer a laundry service; it will be more expensive, although it can be more convenient, as you just drop at reception or get room service to pick up and deliver.

When packing clothes, try to take older items of clothing, if you see new ones in the markets that appeal, discard an older clothing item to save on extra weight in your luggage. Purchase the lightest weighing carry-on bag. There is no point in having a seven to ten-kilogram weight limit on check-in luggage and your bag weighs five kilograms. I will wear my heaviest clothes to and from the airport and onto the flight, jeans, shoes, socks, shirt, and jacket, these weigh the most but are not counted in your flight luggage weigh-ins. If your concern is overheating when you arrive, do not be concerned as transport to and from airports is normally in an air-conditioned vehicle. If you visit a chilly region, you will have your jacket and jeans and shoes to keep you warm. Air conditioning whilst travelling in public transport can be cranked up to full blast. It can get cold, so your jacket will come in handy.

It is, of course, different for ladies, taking swimmers, shorts, sarongs, light flowing dresses, and light tops as a good grouping of suitable clothing in warm climates with the warmer, heavier clothes worn on the flight. Ladies tend to want (require) more toiletries than most male travellers. If you cannot fit them in your bag, then you can always purchase at each destination for low prices.

You will need to pack electronic devices and chargers. These days, with such high technology in smartphones, a camera is not required, however, you will need your phone charger. I recommend that you pack a lightweight power board, these weight only a few grams and allow you to charge more than one device at a time. Purchase a universal socket adaptor that will allow you to plug in and charge any device, in any country. If you are ever in need of a charge for a device and you do not have access to charger, it is possible to plug in your phone to the USB socket on the back of the room TV, if you have your USB cord. The charge will be slower than usual but at least you have a few bars until you get to your charger.

Minimum packing requirements include four or five changes of clothing, a pair of light footwear, toiletries, and electronic chargers in your carry-on bag. Ensure this bag is within required carry-on load weights and size restrictions. A further hint is to roll clothes into tube shapes, to fit in so much more.

CURRENCY CONVERSION

"IT IS ALL TOO CONFUSING"

One of the most confusing topics people will deal with when they travel overseas is currency options.

- How much cash do I take and is it safe?
- Do I just use my credit card?
- Where do I change my money?
- Do I change my money before I go to the airport or when I arrive?
- Can I use ATMs, EFTPOS machines and use PayWave?

Plus, many more questions.

Remember to check the currency used in the areas you will be visiting. Below are the currency types of the countries in the region.

Vietnam (Dong) but they are equally happy to use US dollars.

Cambodia (Riel) will allow you to pay in US dollars and local currency but will nearly always give you change in local currency.

Thailand (Baht)

Malaysia (Ringgit)

Indonesia (Rupiah)

Singapore (Singapore Dollar)

It is important to be aware that where countries use the US dollar, they will accept only crisp, new notes. If you have a note with creases, tears, writing on the note, they will not be accepted. Large-denomination notes like $50USD and $100USD will be difficult to change so the preference is smaller value notes. If you attempt to pay with large value notes in local currency or US currency, especially in markets, getting change will be problematic. In the future sections I discuss using Money Exchanges. Please note that you may get a better exchange rate if you use larger denomination notes when changing money.

WHAT TO TAKE?

During my last month-long trip, I took $1,500. Before departure, I went to a local money exchange and only changed a further $100 into the currency of the country of my first port of call, I then had local currency for taxis and incidentals. **never** change money at airports, the exchange rate is so low, I have witnessed a $0.10c or worse deviation from official quoted rates to offered rates at airport kiosks.

To illustrate the possible losses that can occur with airport money exchange, assume you are departing Vietnam, travelling via Malaysia, back to Australia with a wallet full of Vietnamese Dong. Whilst in transit at an airport in Malaysia, you want to change the Vietnamese Dong into Australian currency. They will first convert the Vietnamese Dong into Malaysian ringgits at poor rates and of course charge a fee, then convert Malaysian ringgits into Australian currency adding more fees and poor rates. This is common practice all over the world, not isolated to this region.

My advice is to use your unspent local currency left over before departure, to part pay your hotel bill. I normally use my credit card to pay hotel bills, but I part pay with unspent local cash and paying the balance with a credit card. You will save on conversion rates on the balance due, and of course, as your credit card charges you an overseas currency conversion fee, you will get another saving. Some hotels also charge a credit card usage fee, this strategy will lessen this cost. If you need to buy something at the airport, just use your EFTPOS card you may pay a small fee, but it is much better than dealing with airport conversion rates.

MONEY EXCHANGE

The best place to change your money when overseas is normally local money exchanges. Ask at your hotel where to locate the money exchange area. There will be more than one shop grouped together, and they will be competing, and you will get a better rate. Your hotel will often have a money exchange service. This may be comparable. Check their rates and compare. It is often found that in the local exchange districts, the rate is as good if not better than the official rates. Only exchange a portion of your currency into the first country's currency. If you need more then you know where to locate the vendor. Secure the balance in your room safe, if you do not feel secure with this option, ask to deposit in the hotel safe. Many travel insurance policies cover you for loss or theft of cash up to $3,000. If insured, you are covered. Check your travel insurance policy to confirm.

A common question is regarding whether cash or card is the best option. I believe both cash and card will serve you during your trip. Your EFTPOS and debit cards will work in most

ATMs around the world and instructions are normally clear. I would advise that you use them in a public place, of course, this same advice applies everywhere. Do not flash your money around. Make yourself familiar with the currency, the colour, and the size of the notes and coins. Local currency exchanges hold a bad reputation as a place to be careful of possible scams. In some cases, this is warranted, but with a little precaution, risks can be reduced and avoided. When you enter a Money Exchange Centre, the rates will normally be on display in full view on a board or a digital screen. Compare the rates with other exchange shops and select the best rate. It is okay to try to barter here; just ask them if they can do better, you have nothing to lose. Inform the staffer how much you wish to convert. They will either, on a calculator or in writing, show you the converted rate and ask if you are happy, (I normally have made that calculation, before entering a transaction) Before leaving with your new currency, **count it**. Count it in front of them and depart when you are happy.

COINS/ NOTES

When buying goods and services, you will at times be given coins in your change. In Cambodia however, whilst coins are minted, they are rarely in circulation. Expect coins in Malaysia, Singapore, Vietnam, and Thailand. Carry a small coin bag for these coins. Although coins have a perceived small value, it is amazing how useful these coins can be when catching trains or buses, or if you are provided with a good service, a couple of coins can be a fitting reward. I tend to leave my unspent coins in my hotel room after departure, to thank the cleaning staff for doing a great job in housekeeping.

In Cambodia, you will get back in change (when paying in US dollars), lots of small local currency notes, commonly, 100-, 200-, 500- and 1000-Riel notes Your wallet will soon bulge with all these notes. Tipping, while common, is not compulsory. It is however nice to reward those who provide you with great service, I tend to use all the small notes that I get, in change, as tips, it will be appreciated by the locals.

During your trip, you may run out of cash. Just go to an ATM, withdraw cash in the local currency.

BUYING AND BARTERING

WHEN TO BUY?

When travelling, we spend money on a variety of things. Clothing, gifts for friends, souvenirs, trinkets, or jewellery items that have caught your eye, to name but a few. Of course, whatever you purchase will be determined by your budget, it is also important to remember, that whatever you buy, you must carry.

Goods on sale in most markets and shops are virtually the same in every city. You will see the same t-shirts, sporting clothing representing world-famous sporting clubs, shorts, watches, wallets, and jewellery in every location. Not too long-ago DVDs and CDs (mostly pirated copies) were on sale in every market. You can still find them, but with streaming services abounding they are not so popular. You can buy belts, shoes, caps, and hats with the same logos in most countries. My tip is to buy desired goods at my last destination. There is no point purchasing early and carrying them with you from country to country.

Do keep in mind, however, that whilst the prices are exceptionally low when compared to home, wherever the cost of living in the lowest, here you will find the lowest prices. I have found Cambodia and Laos, to be among the cheapest places to purchase items. Vietnam, Thailand, and Malaysia are slightly more expensive, but still low compared to home. Your itinerary will determine the best place to buy. The price difference will be only about $1-2USD per piece on low-cost items, so if you love a T-shirt no matter where you are and are prepared to carry it or swap out an older clothing item.... buy it. If you wish to buy a larger and heavier item, most shops can arrange international freight. Of course, every country has their unique cultural souvenirs, you will have to buy, before you leave that country.

Cheap drinks in Pub Street, Siem Reap.

Busy markets

Little India, Georgetown Penang, Malaysia

BARTERING

How do we buy things in Asia? That sounds like a simple question with a simple answer. In Asia, it is the custom to haggle or barter when shopping. This can be quite foreign to people coming from western cultures. It is the norm and a way of life in Asia. A simple rule of thumb is… *if it has no price, you can haggle or barter.* The exception is the purchase of food and drink in cafes and bars and shopping in major department stores. There are some basic suggestions you need to take on board before you start to barter. Firstly, know the currency rate and its value in comparison to your home currency. Shopkeepers will ask you where you live. They are not just being friendly they are fishing for information. They will quote prices in the local currency, instantly converting it back to US dollars or back into your local currency. If you are not aware of the exchange rate you may be confused and deceived.

It is also a good practice before you start to barter for goods, to know the price that you will pay at home for similar items. If you see an item that would normally cost you $50 in your own country (remembering that it is probably a fake or knock-off reproduction), you will not want to pay anything like the full price.

BARTERING TECHNIQUES.

Decide what you are prepared to pay for that item (let us assume for this exercise that $10 is your rock bottom price). As your looking and showing interest in the goods, the shopkeeper will come up to you extolling the great value of the goods. They may even ask you a little bit about where you are from, where you have been, and where you are going next on your trip. This information is important to the shopkeeper. If you tell them that you are on the last days of your holiday, then they know you are more inclined to buy your souvenirs today. If they know you are travelling to a country next, where the goods are dearer, they have some bargaining power by letting you know that their prices will be cheaper than your next location. Answer, by saying *"I am loving your country but leaving in a few days for Cambodia or Laos"*, where they know the goods are cheaper, you can let them know that you also know, that it is cheaper in your next location, and they will need to give you a good price to buy today.

Next, ask the shopkeeper *"What's your best price?"* Assuming the goods, normally sell for around $50 (at home), you can expect a price in his local currency around $30, the plan here is to, after bargaining, sell to you at half the first price (that is about $15), based on the first quote. The psychology here is, that after you have bartered down to half the first price, that will be perceived as a win-win situation. The shopkeeper makes a large margin profit, and you think they dropped the price by 50 per cent.

Your first reply response, after the first price is especially important, I suggest acting very amused by the price. Counter the price by suggesting you will pay in local currency the equivalent of $2. The reaction to that will be a look of horror, remember this is all part of the show. Say something like, *"I only wanted to pay $2 for that"*. They will say *"you're too low"*. Counter by saying *"well you started too high"*. Smile and say, *"let us start again"*. It is important to remember here, no shopkeeper will sell you an item if they will be losing money on that item. The only exemption is when you may be buying extra items and they are prepared to lose on one to gain on a second item.

Let me illustrate a scenario (SK = Shopkeeper, Y = You)

SK:The quote starts at 30.

Y: Start at 2.

SK: Next price drop to 20.

(**SK** wants you to raise your price to 10.)

Y: Remember your bottom line is 10. If you go to 10 straight away, you have no room to move. If you raise to 10, he will say *"meet in the middle"* and try to do a deal at 15. He got the price he wanted from the beginning.
Counter by moving up from 2 to 5.

If you are happy to pay 10 (at this stage) and he is not moving in price, say *"10 last offer"*.

If he says no.... walk away.
Two things will happen. He will follow you or call you back and accept your offer, or offer a new price.

If he does not make a counteroffer or not call you back, then he has reached his price limit.
    You then have a choice, accepting his best price or trying somewhere else.

BUYING TIPS AND SCAMS

I have heard stories from other travellers of markets where most store holders work for a small number of owners. When you purchase goods, they place the goods in different coloured bags. Each colour denotes the skill of the shopper to other vendors, identifying bartering skills, possible easy targets, and warning of hard sales. Try to place purchases in another bag or backpack.

Know the local words for "too expensive" (See later chapter). This is a sign to the shopkeeper that you may not be an easy target. Shopkeepers of Chinese origin, believe it is good luck for the first customer of the day to make a purchase. If you go early to a market and encounter a Chinese shopkeeper, they will be very keen to make sure that you purchase if you are first through the door that day. Multi purchasing items, buying more than one of the same items, can help get a better price. If you are buying more than one, do not tell the shopkeeper of this intention at the beginning of the transaction. Start by getting the best price you can for one item. Next, ask for a better price if you buy two. I once brought nine pairs of sunglasses as gifts. I started with a price for one pair, got a better price for two, asked how much if I bought four. Each time getting a better price. I increased to eight and was offered a better per-item price. Increased, lastly to nine and was incredibly pleased with the result.

TOURS

When experiencing new destinations for the first time, get out and see the country, the town, the region, try the foods, meet the locals, visit the attractions, and embrace the culture.

BOOKING TOURS

Please consult a map, do a little online research, get yourself to these locations. In some cases, this is the best and cheapest option. However, in some cases, you have no option but to pay for and join a tour group. On my first trip to Asia, I did the research, booked all my tours from the comfort of my home. All these tours were great. I found on arrival, that I had paid well over local acquired prices.

In Hanoi, a short walk from my hotel in the Old Quarter I found a street lined with tour companies, their tours and prices were in many cases up to 70% less than I paid before leaving on my journey. Of course, do your research, decide where you want to go, what you want to see, where you want to visit. On arrival, firstly, get a price from your hotel, then visit local tour providers, compare, and take the best deal. You will not miss out on a place by waiting until you arrive. If you are travelling during a major public holiday or festival period prebooking may be important due to crowds. Booking locally with a tour operator or your hotel will allow you to tap into the local knowledge.

I have walked around Angkor Wat in Cambodia, with a tour operator and solo on a second visit. The temple complex at Angkor is awe-inspiring at any time, and the little snippets of information you get from a professional guide can make all the difference. Quite often, when I have a professional guide, I note solo travellers following a few metres behind, listening in on the information provided by my guide.

I find independently travelling to some historical sites has its downside. They are often a distance out of main city areas, taxi drivers and tuk-tuk drivers are happy to give a great price to get you there, but the prices seem to double when you want to get back. You normally have little or no alternative services for return transport. If you can negotiate a return price that may work for you, but if you're relying on taxi services or tuk-tuk drivers they seem to have all worked out a great profitable return price, you will not get a discount by going from driver to driver.

The local tour operators are also a wealth of information regarding other things in their city or region. They usually are only too happy to give you advice on restaurants, places of interest or anything else that will get you staying longer or spending extra. When booking tours which include travelling long distances on buses, ask if a VIP bus is available, this will ensure you have air conditioning, Wi-Fi and probably a lot more legroom and comfortable seating.

FREE TOURS

Whenever arriving for the first time in a new city, arrange a free walking tour. These are readily available in nearly every city in the world, and they are free. Free walking guides commonly are currently studying International Studies or English language, wishing to practice their English skills and of course, proud of their city. The only costs you may incur are public transport tickets for yourself and the guide if applicable. Offer the guide a cold drink or a meal if you are having a meal break whilst out exploring. At the end of the tour, you can give them a tip.

Bayon Temple ruins, Siem Reap, Cambodia

Sometimes these will be one-on-one tours and other times a group tour, either way, they normally run for about three to four hours. They will either, meet you at your hotel or a central location, they will show you the local points of interest, answer your questions and will introduce you to their city. Normally, you will only fleetingly visit places of interest on a free tour. Often, I return to these locations on another day to take my time and fully explore. Some of these free walking tour guides have become great friends after meeting on the tour and a wealth of information going forward. Normally, I book a free walking tour for the first morning after arrival. I then get a feel of the city, ask them questions that come to mind. Where is the best place to eat? Where is the best coffee? Where is the best place to get a drink? They are amazing sources of information.

TOUR TIMING

Before you book a holiday anywhere in the world, check that you are not arriving during any major festivals, public holidays, or national days of importance. The crowds on these days can be enormous and overwhelming. Even on a pupil-free day, children or family orientated attractions are extremely overcrowded.

We once booked a trip to Hong Kong, planning to arrive in the first week of October, before finalising flights and accommodation, we checked out national holidays in the area, finding that the first week in October is a major holiday period for the Chinese people and over ten million Chinese visitors flock to countries close to their borders. Hong Kong prices increase, and availability is limited. We were advised that theme parks and attractions would be very overcrowded, and we rescheduled. Travel dates were revised to arrive in Hong Kong a week later and we missed all those problems.

Visitors are also concerned about when is the optimal time of the year to travel. The temperature does not change too much in most parts of Thailand, Cambodia, Malaysia, and Southern Vietnam with temperatures reaching over 30°C for most days in summer and winter. Humidity is high during the wet season. You will notice a build-up of storm clouds and some of the heaviest downpours you will ever witness. The rain will come in waves with time to continue wandering and time to duck for cover as a rain burst nears. It will clean the streets and gutters and refresh the day. In Hanoi, as it is away from the equator, it will get colder during winter months with snow at Sapa and the surrounding mountains possible. You may have to go into a market and buy a knockoff winter jacket for a bargain if you are not prepared. I have travelled in the region at all times of the year and the weather has never diminished my enjoyment.

When you have a great tuk-tuk driver he will take you to the non-crowded side of Angkor Wat, avoiding thousands of other travelers and the gate opens at the same time so you have the place to yourself until you meet the crowds around halfway. Thank you, Monday Hong.

CULTURAL ADVICE

When visiting countries, it is important to keep in mind, different cultural and religious practices. Indonesia and Malaysia are predominantly Muslim countries and Ramadan is one of the most important periods for the local population. It does not have too much effect on your visit, although it is important to acknowledge and be mindful of not offending. In Muslim countries, it may be difficult getting a taxi mid-afternoon as they may be delayed with many drivers at prayer.

Water puppetry, Hanoi

HOTEL TRANSFERS, TAXIS AND TUK-TUKS

HOTEL TRANSFERS

It is one of the most comforting experiences is to walk out of the arrivals lounge, see your name either on a laptop screen or a simple piece of A4 paper, telling you that you have arrived, and someone is here to take you to your hotel. It is a little luxury cost I am happy to pay. Your bags will be carried directly to an air-conditioned vehicle with no need to haggle for a price. You know you are going straight to your hotel and the holidays have begun.

I know that you do not have to do this, and in some cases, where I am familiar with the city and surroundings, I use the taxi service or book an online car, like Uber or Grab. In most countries today, Uber or its equivalent are available. Book your transport to the airport at a much-reduced price compared to taxi or hotel transfers. You can even book on arrival at the airport and go to the Uber pickup area to meet your driver. As always, remember you are on holiday, so why not treat yourself.

TAXI SERVICES

In Malaysia, they have a safe and pre-priced taxi service system at all major airports. After clearing customs and picking up your luggage (if you are carrying any), you visit the taxi service desk. Advise the staff of your required destination, pay a set price, then take your receipt to the kerbside taxi staff. They will call up a vehicle that suits the needs of your travelling party, give half the receipt to the driver, which includes the destination. You are on your way.

In Cambodia, most hotels include in your booking, a free airport pickup – take advantage of this offer. In Vietnam and Thailand, I normally get the hotel pick up service to collect me on arrival. I realise it is a lot cheaper to get a local bus, or you could haggle a price with a taxi driver and save money. Consider that the bus is not always waiting for you and some waiting time will be required. You will also be carrying luggage which may be problematic on a public bus or train. The route of the public transport may not be direct to your accommodation, so you may have to still, get a taxi or other local transport.

Taxi ranks can be very crowded places. You may be in a long queue and must negotiate a price. The comfort and convenience of a hotel transfer are well worth the cost. When returning to the airport, either ask the hotel to provide a vehicle and this cost will be included in your hotel bill, or for a cheaper option try Uber or a ride share option or advise the doorman to call a taxi. Ask the hotel staff for an estimate of a fair price. Confirm this price is acceptable to the driver before departure.

A further option to save, is on departure day, if not departing on an early flight, book a tour before your departure time. Ask the tour operator to end the tour at the airport, saving you a return trip cost.

GETTING AROUND

Once you arrive and you are starting to negotiate the streets and the area close to your accommodation, my first suggestion, as suggested earlier, is a free walking tour to get your bearings. Follow up with an independent walk around the area noting places to eat, transport hubs, convenience stores and other places of interest. Make note of landmarks like tall buildings

Golden Bridge, Ba Na Hills, Sunworld Resort Da Nang Vietnam

and billboards so that you can navigate back to your hotel with ease. I always ask for a hotels business card and keep it in my wallet. If you ever get lost or are just too tired or too hot to walk, give the card to a driver and it will get you back to your hotel.

Earlier, I mentioned keeping coins. If you decide to catch local buses or train systems, coins speed up your payment options. In major cities with a light rail or train system, you can buy a multi-pass at any station. In many places, hiring of bicycles, scooters, and vehicles, are available.

You will need to invest in an international licence which you can purchase before departing. Hiring a car with a driver is the safest option as traffic rules and the quality of the roads can make driving hazardous. I have heard said that road rules are merely a suggestion in some places. Depending on your place of origin, cars may be travelling on the opposite side of the road to what you are accustomed to. The sound of the car horn will become a constant chorus as you walk and travel near roadways, as it is used as a courtesy and safety tool and not a show of rage.

Bicycle hire is safe and convenient in less built-up areas. Many motorbike and scooter hire companies will offer you insurance, but this insurance commonly only covers the cost of any damage to their equipment. It does not cover injury to yourself or others. Your travel insurance will only cover you if you are operating a vehicle that you have a licence to operate in your country of residence. If you do not have a bike licence, then you cannot **legally** ride a bike, therefore you certainly will not be insured for any injuries that you may sustain. In Australia, you do not need a licence to ride a scooter under 50cc, but it is so difficult to find a scooter under 50cc in Asia. Most are 125cc or higher so do not take the risk unless you have a licence, or the driver has a licence. Check with your travel insurance provider before you depart to ensure you know whether you covered or not. Police also tend to target foreign drivers even if you are obeying perceived road rules.

TUK-TUKS AND OTHER LOCAL OPTIONS

While each country has a taxi fleet willing to take you anywhere, most also have a secondary fleet of open-air transport. They are most commonly called tuk-tuks in Thailand and Cambodia, cyclos in Vietnam, and trishaws in Malaysia with other varieties in other places. Some will be motor powered; others use leg power to get you to your destination. Some cities have open-air, brightly painted pick-up vans that ferry you around the city. When you decide to use a taxi, tuk-tuk or other modes of transport, your first question should be whether they will be operating a meter. Mostly, taxis do not have meters or are unwilling to use them. Inform them of your required destination. Ask the price. I tend to ask hotel staff or locals how much it will cost to go between destinations and then I tell the driver that is how much I will pay.

Your conversation could sound like...

"I will pay you $2 to take me to the temple is that okay with you?"

On acceptance hop in and enjoy the ride.

If the driver replies…

"No, $2 is not enough."

Then tell him *"That is what we paid yesterday. Why is it more expensive today? Well, no problem. I will find someone else."*

If your price is fair then they will most likely agree, if not, ask how much extra, if not unreasonable go for it. As mentioned earlier if you are returning from a location out of town with limited other transport options the price to return will be higher and you may have to just accept. It is all about supply and demand.

The streets of Georgetown Penang by Tri-shaw

When in Cambodia, especially in places like Siem Reap, you can engage a tuk-tuk driver for the duration of your stay. It is like having a tour guide and a vehicle for personal use, it is normally very reasonable. Give him a generous tip on top, as his price will surprise. The driver will be outside your hotel waiting for you, taking you to restaurants (we always offered him a meal) or waiting to take you to your next tourist location.

In places like Georgetown, on the island of Penang, Malaysia they have Tri-shaws that will ferry you around the UNESCO-listed city, pre-covid it cost around 50 ringgits for 2 hours – great transport and a fun tour as well.

In Vietnam, some taxi companies are government-owned, and drivers tend to use meters more than in other countries. Also in Vietnamese cities, Uber or its equivalent, Grab, is a choice between mainly green helmeted riders on scooters and in cars. If you are not solo you may need two bikes. It is ridiculously cheap and because we know that it gets hot in Asia, after wandering around for hours in plus 35°C degree heat, it feels good to just jump on the back of a scooter, or feel the airflow as you ride in a tuk-tuk and be taken back to your hotel.

The crazy traffic in Hanoi, but it works. Good luck crossing the road.

TRAFFIC AND CROSSING THE ROAD

Depending on the country the mode of transport varies. Vietnam seems to be run on the back of scooters and motorbikes. In Thailand, Malaysia and Singapore, cars trucks and buses dominate. In Cambodia it is a combination of both. No matter where you are, crossing the street can be hazardous.

Five on a bike, very common sight

Where cars, buses and trucks dominate, try to find overpasses or pedestrian walkways. In Vietnam, where two wheels are king, the streets are full of hundreds upon hundreds of bikes. The simplest way to cross the street is to **just cross the street**. I know that sounds simplistic, and it can be very scary the first time you cross a Vietnamese street, but after a while, you will get used to it. My advice is to try, walk at a constant pace and **do not stop**, the bikes will move around you. Watch a few locals first, to get the concept and to build up your bravery before you step out. Try and get eye contact with the closest bike rider and he or she will move to either side of you and then just keep on going and they all will do that. Do not step out if a bus, car or taxi is coming. Wait for bikes. The good news is that roads are so full of bikes and other vehicles then traffic is not travelling at fast speeds, so they have plenty of time to manoeuvre around you. Good luck.

FOOD

Your fondest memories when travelling overseas will be the different foods you can try, sample and taste. Each country has their special cuisines, unique ways of preparing foods, and varieties in taste, spice, and ingredients, making your food tour as exciting as any other part of your holiday. We in the western regions of the world are used to certain styles of food, certain ingredients, and manners of eating with different utensils and different styles of venues.

Pub Street Siem Reap

WHERE AND WHAT TO EAT

So where do you eat when you are on holiday in Asia? Wander any street, you will be confronted with so many choices, so many sights, so many smells that your eyes and mouth will get excited or even offended. Every country has an abundance of street food and in most cases, delicious, healthy, and safe, if you take a few precautions.

I have a few simple rules that I follow whenever travelling. I have never contracted any of the stomach issues of which Asia is unfairly famous. We all have heard about "Bali belly" or "Bangkok belly" or "Hanoi's revenge" with growing trepidation about eating local food. But if you follow my simple rules, you can avoid most of the issues. Remember it is not uncommon to get food poisoning in your local home city.

Firstly, do not drink the water, that sounds simple enough. Bottled water is cheap and abundant, most hotels leave free bottles in your room every day and stores are selling water for a few cents a bottle. We do forget that ice is made of water and put into your drinks. The ice may not be made from filtered or clean water. If this is the case, you may be in for some problems. If you wish to avoid ice altogether, only drink bottled or canned drinks wherever you dine or buy drinks. In the many regularly frequented cafes, bars, and restaurants the ice is made from filtered water. Ask, if you do not see signs informing you.

The advent of social media has assisted in keeping you healthy. Once a venue is reviewed by patrons and they link it to getting ill, it is panned on sites like TripAdvisor or similar. This will seriously affect the store's profitability. They will then ensure they have a healthy ice option.

I am very careful in wet markets and roadside pop-up stores. Here if you buy a drink, you can be offered an unchilled can, and will be offered an accompanying glass of ice to chill your drink. Vendors in wet markets do not have huge overheads and as they mainly cater for local customers, they tend to make the ice at home from local water supplies and are not safe for tourists. Sadly, if you are very thirsty, you should consume the warm can of drink.

The famous Banh Mi

Secondly, eat street food, but do not eat street food where you are not sure how long ago it was cooked. If you do buy as an example, satay sticks at a street vendor, ensure the chicken was cooked in front of you, then it should be okay to eat. A good sign is if you see a line-up of people at that same vendor then you know that the food is not sitting around too long and should be okay, but if you see a pile of uneaten product, warming and limited customers, then maybe it is possible that it has been too long since cooking and maybe a problem. Sometimes they part cook and will finish when you order, this should be fine. It must be remembered that we normally go out to eat at mealtimes, this means that the vendors are busy, and food is fresh and safe.

Rule three is quite simple: if you do not like the look of it, or the ingredients are not what you would normally eat, do not eat it. In Cambodia, for example, you will find vendors selling all types of insects and snakes and other reptiles for you to try. If you want to have a taste it is up to you if you do not, just avoid it. Take a picture and move on.

FOOD LIKE HOME

With the many western tourists that now travel to Asia, lots of western food items are for sale. I have travelled with younger family members, who have ordered pizza on numerous occasions. I have found that after travelling for a period you crave some western food and there is nothing wrong with ordering a great burger and fries for a change.

If you require certain dietary options such as gluten-free foods or your choice is vegan or vegetarian, you will find you are catered for with many choices. Inform tour operators if you have a meal in any tour option so your preferred choices are available.

The food you eat is always a matter of choice, I do not like my food very spicy others love as much chilli or spices they can get. Be aware, our tender Western stomachs sometimes are not happy with our choices.

I once heard a comedian in Australia say on stage, that it was great to be home from Asia because he missed having solid bowel motions. We all laughed, but there was an element of truth in his words. Your body is accustomed to certain types of food and fibres in your food. It does affect how your body acts and reacts with your basic bodily functions. Do not worry too much, it is quite normal. I will admit that one of my essential items on a trip is to pack a box of Gastro-Stop from my local pharmacy. Cost less than $10 and it gives piece of mind. Please consult your doctor before departure to get the best option for you personally.

WATER AND DRINKING

Always purchase a large bottle of water and keep it in the bathroom of your hotel room.

Use this bottle for cleaning teeth, rinsing your mouth, washing toothbrushes, and taking any medication without using the local tap water. We do not live here permanently; our bodies have not built-up immunities to local bacteria and when you clean your teeth if you are using tap water you can unwittingly be exposed. Alcohol is cheap and abundant throughout Asia. Different types of beers are brewed in different countries, and you can get every type of cocktail you can imagine (very cheaply). Normal dangers do apply when drinking alcohol and overindulging. Wine is available but mostly imported so it can be costly. Vietnam does have a small wine industry and you can purchase in selected venues.

Just love the many comic signs throughout Asia.

Western wine lovers may prefer to wait till they get home, to enjoy a glass of wine. (I have tried the Vietnamese red wine and whilst not my favourite wine, it is okay). Many of the markets and street food vendor areas turn into nightclubs and bars later in the evening with their inherent dangers, but if you are careful and aware then you will have a great night.

One of the great traditions in Vietnam is Ba Hoi. You will find these little sidewalk bars with small plastic stools on many corners in most cities of Vietnam. The beer is brewed daily can cost less than 20 cents a plastic glass. You will get to meet the locals and after a few beers, language will not be an issue. Lots of laughter, so one piece of advice is, if you are over 90 kilos, put two chairs together or you might fall off laughing in the streets.

Sunset drinks on the beach in Langkawi, Malaysia

LOCAL FOOD OPTIONS

In some countries, due to religious traditions, certain foods are not readily available. If you are in a Muslim country, pork products will not be available, which means turkey bacon with your eggs for breakfast. If you are lucky enough to be in a city where Buddhist monks parade in the morning to collect alms and food offerings, ask a local vendor if you can purchase something to give to the monks and you will get a blessing for your good deed.

Banh Mi, (up close) great Vietnamese street food.

I normally book hotels where buffet breakfasts are included in my accommodation costs. I have a hearty breakfast before venturing out for the day. Having toured and explored, find an air-conditioned café, have a leisurely lunch before heading back to the pool or the AC. Venture back out again after dark when it has cooled down, ready for your dinner. Outside street bars and cafes are great in the evening or food hawker centres, food courts and street food. You tend to eat more when on holidays. The food is healthy, and you do lots of walking and sweating (it is hot in Asia) so I have never put on any weight on any trip to Asia (maybe I am just lucky).

Every time I have been away, I have noted that when I return, I keep looking for my chopsticks for the first few days. I recommend when visiting Asia to organise a local cooking class. One of my travelling companions was a vegetarian, so we booked a vegetarian cooking class in Chiang Mai, Thailand. I informed the trainer that I was not a vegetarian and she happily told me when to include meat products in every dish if I wished to cook a non-vegetarian meal when I was home. I highly recommend cooking classes while travelling. Some hotels do offer them but if not, they are readily available everywhere.

Happy eating.

Mango with Sticky Rice

MEDICAL AND MEDS

TAKING MEDICATION WITH YOU

If you are on any type of medication before you travel overseas, then it is perfectly legal to take your prescription medication with you. The precautions you need to take are quite small. You will need to have a letter from your doctor noting the medications you are taking and keep the medication in the original box (showing your name, date of prescription and dosage). This is particularly important if your medication is psychotropic or strong painkillers. Procession of certain drugs is illegal in most countries unless under a prescription from a doctor. One of my travelling companions had several items of medication, so we carried a letter every trip, as is required under law. Never were we asked to provide evidence, at no time did a customs officer ask to inspect medication, and all medication was packed in a toiletry bag, not concealed. At no time were we questioned during the trip, but it will happen at one time, so it is important to be fully compliant and legal.

MEDICATION ASSISTANCE

I have on occasions, been unwell, as in minor cold symptoms whilst being overseas. I was able to go to a pharmacist and get medication to ease my symptoms. I have on one occasion visited a doctor, whilst in Penang, Malaysia, with an ear problem. The medical centre was very efficient and fixed the problem very quickly, for a cost of around 50 ringgits (about $15) Earlier, it was mentioned that I usually take some Gastro-Stop as a precaution. It is advisable to take paracetamol or ibuprofen if you use these items regularly. These over-the-counter medications are readily available, as well as most cold and flu remedies.

I have noticed that pharmacists in some countries can provide prescription medication without a prescription, although they do dispense limited amounts. It is not advisable to purchase prescription medication without appropriate medical advice. If you are unwell while overseas your first option is to contact the hotel reception. They will have contacts with foreign speaking medical assistance. Keep all paperwork and receipts to assist with travel insurance claims. Many travel insurance companies provide a 24-hr hotline to policyholders to assist in any emergency.

MEDICAL HOLIDAY

It is a common practice to have medical procedures done in Asia, the cost factor alone can be attractive. Ensure you do your research before committing to any procedure.

I visit an optometrist in Malaysia and have had glasses made for me, as well as eye tests on three separate occasions, at a very reduced price to costs at home and 24-hour turn-around. I have also visited a dentist in Hoi An, Vietnam and had a crown done at 10% of the cost at home. The dental surgery I attended used brand-new equipment, and US-trained dentists. I have had no issues post-work. As mentioned earlier, if you are going to do any medical procedures while in Asia, I suggest you do your research. Not all operators are up to Australian or western standards.

PHONES AND DATA.

YOUR PHONE

It is rare to travel anywhere in the world these days without having a trusty smartphone on hand. It is your camera, your diary, your communication means to loved ones, holds your ticketing arrangements, hotel accommodation data, GPS and maps, stores your pictures, memories, your payment method, and on occasions provides a light in the dark. It has become an essential travel companion.

I have one of the latest smartphones, but when I go overseas, I take my previous smartphone (over 2 years old). If I lose it or it is stolen, it is covered by my travel insurance, and I have not lost my newest phone. The camera is still particularly good and all you need while travelling. In essence, its main function is to take those photos, communicate either online with family and friends, post your photos on social media, use as a map to get you around, or out of trouble when you are lost.

Use it as a tool, but you will miss seeing wonders if you are looking down at your phone all day while on holiday. I recommend downloading an app called Maps.ME. You can download the places you are going to visit, before leaving using free data from home. It works without having a Wi-Fi connection, provided you have downloaded the location. I also suggest you take a photo of your passport, your birth certificate and any other I.D. you may need. If the worst-case scenario happens and you lose your passport, information stored will assist the closest Embassy or Consulate to have you issued with a replacement passport as soon as possible. Email all the pictures and I.D. data to yourself so it is easily accessible from any device.

WI-FI AND DATA

Connecting to Wi-Fi services is one of the most vital, modern-day endeavours whilst travelling. I have never purchased data in Asia because I have always found it readily available for FREE... Nearly every café and bar has free Wi-Fi, with passwords normally displayed on tables or signage in plain sight. Ask the service staff if they have Wi-Fi and their private, free password.

Most hotels and hostels throughout Asia provide free Wi-Fi for guests. You can do all your downloading, all your chatting with friends, all your updating your social media status in your hotel or having a drink or meal in a cafe.

Many public transport vehicles have Wi-Fi, you are never too far away from a Wi-Fi service. Most airports allow you to connect to their free Wi-Fi, waiting for a plane or just arrived you can log on to the airport Wi-Fi, allowing you to contact a hotel, order an Uber or just tell someone you have arrived safely. Depending on your phone plan, you may have options (paying a little bit extra) allowing your phone service to work when overseas. My phone company now has offered, the use of my phone and my contracted data allowance, while roaming for a temporary fee. Check with your service provider to be advised of your options. when in doubt place your phone setting to airplane mode.

TRAVEL HINTS

TRAVEL INSURANCE

For the first two years of travel, I used a private travel insurance company. I recommend you research which company suits your needs. I used World Nomads as they were reasonably priced, environmentally friendly and I liked that part of my premium was donated to worthy causes. I did make a claim with World Nomads and found them quite easy to deal with – my claim was processed quickly, and I received my compensation in a short time.

For the last few years, I have been able to access free travel insurance connected to my bank's credit card. I contacted them to talk about the policy and found it like my previous paid policy. At this stage, I have not made a claim with my bank's free travel insurance. The only condition is that my card required I spent $500 on my trip using the card before departure. I am not endorsing any company only detailing my experiences. If you have a similar arrangement with your credit card provider, check their policy statement to see if it suits your needs.

Due to Covid's presence in the world, check with your insurance companies to see if you are covered and any conditions attached to your policy. There may be conditions regarding vaccines or countries that have a travel ban in place. I am aware that people travel without travel insurance. I believe this is not a wise move. Accidents that require hospitalisation and medical evacuation can cost upwards of $100,000USD plus. Travel insurance is an expense, but it gives peace of mind.

Reclining Buddha, Mekong Region Vietnam

VISAS

Before you travel overseas, check if your country of residency or citizenship requires an entry visa.

On my last trip to Vietnam, one of my travelling companions was travelling on a different passport to mine. I was required to apply and pay for a visa to enter the country whilst my travelling companion was exempt and had free entry. This situation can be reversed, depending on your citizenship, the passport you travel on, and the arrangements between respective countries. It is a simple matter to check online whether you need a visa to enter a particular country and then follow the instructions.

Commonly, a VOA or visa-on-arrival is all that you need. At some entry points, on arrival, you will only need to fill out forms and possibly pay a fee to gain entry. When applying for a visa, you can have a choice of a single-entry visa or multiple entry visas. This will, of course, depend on your itinerary. Most visas are granted for 30 days however you can apply for longer in certain circumstances.

Visa arrangements are different from country to country. In my case, as an Australian citizen, I do not need a prearranged visa for Singapore, Malaysia, and Thailand, I am granted a free 30-day VOA at immigration on arrival. I would need to pay for an entry visa for Cambodia which can be organised on arrival. Check the cost before departure. It will be in USD, and you will not have easy access to ATMs at the airport.

You do need a visa for Vietnam. To enter Vietnam, we have options as Australian citizens. One option is to print out a visa application form, attach credit card details, and post your actual passport to the Vietnamese Consulate in Canberra. At the time of writing, it cost $90, and you needed a prepaid return post bag. Your passport will be returned with Visa attached. The second option is to obtain a letter of invitation to travel to Vietnam. These can be obtained online for around $20, or many tourist companies and hotels can organise one for you before you arrive in Vietnam. Some may charge a fee, some may include it in your costs. Your airline will not let you depart on their flight to Vietnam without this letter of invitation or a pre-arranged visa in your passport. On arrival, you will proceed to the immigration desk, you will produce your passport, your letter of invitation, completed forms, (forms are available online or they have a supply at the desk) two passport size photos and $25USD. This option is ONLY available at international airports and international shipping ports.

This will not be accepted at land crossings. You will need a pre-approved visa in your passport before arrival and crossing into

Vietnam by road. If you are in a neighbouring country, you will need to obtain this at the closest consulate before crossing, if you have not obtained a visa before leaving home. The easiest way to obtain entry is to apply online for an E-visa... Over eighty countries enjoy this option and will allow entry (for less than thirty days) at currently thirty-three entry points. The online process is simple to compete and costs $25USD. Generally, you will get confirmation in three business days and a link to print out a visa approval, to hand in at customs. This method ensures quick entry into Vietnam and saves the risk of mailing your passport and possible mail loss. It must be noted that during covid restrictions this method has been suspended, it is assumed it will be reinstated when restrictions no longer apply.

Cambodia recently added an e--visa option to streamline entry. This option is available for arrivals at Phnom Penh, Siem Reap and Sihanoukville International Airports. The online process is simple to use and will result in you receiving a printable colour visa to staple into a blank page of your passport. It currently costs $36USD. Be aware that there are several unofficial e-visa sites, make sure you are using official government sites.

I have recently read that Thailand is considering an incoming Tourist fee to start in 2022. At present the amount is reported to be 500 Baht. It is reported that this fund with be used to develop new tourism projects. Once this fee is imposed, please keep in mind when visiting the region to be prepared with local currency and if your trip includes multiple entries into Thailand, the choice of visa needs to be considered.

WHO DO YOU TELL YOU ARE GOING OVERSEAS?

Do not forget before you go to any country other than your

own, to notify your bank or banks that you will be accessing banking services whilst overseas. Inform them of the countries you are going to visit including dates of travel. If you fail to do so, your accounts will likely be frozen. The banks will take no chance and freeze your cards, assuming they are being used without your consent. A phone call, back to your bank will fix the problem, but it can be very inconvenient in the short term.

It is important, if you receive any government payments to notify the relevant department, that you intend to go overseas, this may affect your payments. Check with your country's regulations on this matter. The Australian Government through DFAT (Department of Foreign Affairs and Trade) have a travel safe app that is optional, but particularly important to use. This website allows you to give as many details as you can, about your trip and itinerary. If you need to be contacted, the Australian Government can easily make contact. In the case of any natural disasters or any other issues of major importance, it is easy for Australian Consulate staff to assist you or find you. Research the equivalent options in your country.

DOCUMENTS

As I have mentioned earlier, copying identification documents, your passport, and sending copies as an email attachment to yourself, in case you lose your phone or passport, is a great way to ensure you have access to the needed documents to replace a lost passport. This small task can save you time and complications. Any Wi-Fi enabled computer will allow you to access your details and speed up the process of replacing your documents.

Airlines do not provide tickets but produce e-tickets and itineraries with booking numbers. Print these out to make it easier for check-in. In most cases, you only need your passport and a copy of the email showing your booking number. I also print out my hotel reservations. I once booked into a hotel, and they proceeded to asked me if I would like to purchase breakfast each morning. I already had free breakfast included in my booking. I was able to show the printed-out reservation which stated that I had free breakfast included and that problem was solved. The printed reservations also have the address of the hotel which you can show to a taxi driver.

PRE-TRAVEL INSIGHTS

Make yourself aware of important cultural customs that you will encounter on your travels. In certain countries, certain styles of attire may be deemed offensive. Several countries consider lowcut tops and dresses taboo. A dress code is required before you can enter a temple and as a sign of respect, you may need to cover up if not wearing appropriate clothing. In the chapter on food, we highlighted certain foods may not be available due to religious restrictions. A custom to be aware of is the reluctance of some monks to make physical contact with females, only accepting offerings or even handshakes from male tourists, although they are normally happy to give blessings and advice. This is not universal as I have seen monks happy to shake hands with all genders. It is advisable to ask first, before making any physical contact.

Public toilets are plentiful, however may not be up to the same standards you are used to in your own country. Some public toilets may charge a fee. The upside of paying a fee is that these will usually be clean. Be aware that free public toilets may not have any toilet paper, drying towels or blowers and soap. It is recommended to carrying a small pack of wet wipes as they can be used instead of toilet paper and ensuring hygiene when washing your hands.

In many hotel rooms to turn on the power you must insert a tag attached to your keys, this turns on the power and turns it off when removing the tag, saving power costs for the property. This can be a problem if you are charging devices whilst out exploring. Depending on the size of the tag (it is normally credit card sized), place a non-valuable card in its place, for example a loyalty card, and the power will stay on and charge your device. Do not leave a credit card and wait until house cleaning have completed your room for the day.

SCAMS

Among the biggest fears when travelling, is to be a victim of some type of scam. Scammers can be found in every country. Just look in the inbox of your junk-mail to see proof. There is a big difference between being scammed and being overcharged, sometimes when travelling. We cannot help but be overcharged. Look at a price of a cup of coffee or glass of wine in your city to see the huge range from a low cost to a high-cost beverage.

Where the cost of living is low in comparison, what locals consider a larger cost, is to us exceedingly small. In Cambodia, you will commonly find children at tourist attractions, attempting to sell you postcards and other items. These items are very reasonably priced, and it is very tempting to purchase from the children as you may feel sorry for them. Locals have warned me, that if tourists continue to buy from these children, their parents will not send them to school thus depriving them of an education and prosperous future. In Siem Reap, it is quite common to be approached by young girls under twelve years old, carrying a small child, with an empty baby milk bottle, begging you for assistance to buy milk for their hungry baby brother or sister. They normally target western ladies who are overwhelmed with sadness and happy to help. They do not want your cash, instead, they will escort you to a nearby store to buy some milk. The tourist feels like they have helped and leave content, the young girl then goes back into the shop returns the milk back on the shelf and get a rebate from the shopkeeper. The more we enable this, the less likely the children will be educated while they are making an income for their family.

Commonly while wandering around Bangkok, you will be approached by tuk-tuk drivers, offering you a 2-hour tour of the city at extremely low rates. During this tour, you will end up being taken to a jewellery store or something similar. In the store, very persuasive salespeople, will try to sell you gems or such items which most likely will turn out to be nothing near the value if you get appraised on returning home. The drivers get a kickback and free fuel from the stores for bringing in customers.

Remember it is important to always check the money given back to you as change. Make sure that it is correct, be aware of the colour and denomination of local currency as it can be confusing.

Businesses all over the world, strive to maximise profits, it is understandable that vendors in any country and any business will try to get the best price. You will be quoted what they call a tourist price, with the expectation that you will haggle to get a lower price. Never accept the first offer. But you cannot begrudge the locals from trying to making extra profit.

AIRPORTS

Travelling between different countries in Asia means you will be in and out of airports in many countries. I have highlighted several popular, major airports to give you an idea and hints to move through them as quickly and efficiently as possible. Of course, Wi-Fi is always available in airports.

Changi, Singapore.

Changi has been voted the best airport in the world to endure a long-term stopover, I can understand this result. Once current construction is completed, Changi will comprise five major terminals. Each packed with places to wait comfortably, for your next flight. There are duty-free shops, swimming pools, bars, cinemas, showers, eateries, and short-term accommodation. Buses and trains link the terminals, with self-explanatory signage, allowing you to get around without stress. Singapore is connected to the airport by an efficient train service, cheap and punctual. A taxi ride to the city centre will cost you less than $20. As a major hub, you can transit anywhere in the world from Singapore. Food is reasonably priced with lots of choices, although alcohol is expensive. Wi-Fi is freely available in all buildings. High-end, duty-free shopping is also available so enjoy your time at Changi International Airport.

Kuala Lumpur

Kuala Lumpur is serviced by two major airports, namely, Kuala Lumpur International Airport One or KLIA1, which mainly, services full-fare airlines, and Kuala Lumpur International Airport Two or KLIA2, servicing mostly low-cost airlines. Both are modern, and very spacious, but be prepared for long walks to and from departure and arrival lounges. These airports are very spread out, so give yourself plenty of time. Train services connect both airports and on to the city. A taxi service, where you pre-pay at a taxi service desk is available as in most Malaysian airports. It takes sixty minutes to drive from the airports to the centre of the city (more during peak hours) so allow for this travel time. The cost of a taxi is comparable to the cost of two persons on the train, if your group is two or more, a taxi is the cheapest option, and you will be delivered to your hotel directly. Lots of choices with regards to eating and shopping are available whilst in both terminal complexes. Wi-Fi and charging stations are readily available.

Penang International Airport

Whilst an international airport, Penang Airport is nowhere near the size of the airports in capital cities. This makes it easy to navigate and it does not take long to find your departure gate. As in most major Malaysian airports, a prepaid taxi service desk will get you a taxi to take you to your destination. The capital, Georgetown, and the beach area Batu Ferringhi are about 45 minutes to an hour away from the airport depending on traffic conditions.

Views from Penang Hill down to Georgetown.

Bangkok airports

Like Kuala Lumpur, Bangkok is serviced by two international airports. Many low-cost airlines, domestic and a few full-fare airlines operate out of Don Mueang Airport. Most full-fare airlines operate from Suvarnabhumi Airport. Unlike Kuala Lumpur, these airports are not close to each other. A free transit bus operates between the airports. It can take over two hours to travel between the airports by bus. I have travelled by car in a big rush (not recommended) in an hour, luckily without much traffic. Traffic in Bangkok can extend this time considerably. If transiting through Bangkok, ensure you check if you are arriving and departing from different airports. You will need to give yourself ample time to collect luggage, clear customs, and travel between venues. If you are leaving the country again, check-in, clearing customs, and ample time to board your flight is needed. I suggest giving yourself at least five hours between flights to be comfortable. This will allow for any delays and traffic jams. There are numerous options when travelling from either airport into the city with the usual choices of trains, buses, and taxis. Shopping choices and dining choices are available to cater for your needs.

Hanoi (Noi Bai International Airport)

The airport in Hanoi is a modern building situated forty minutes outside of the city depending on traffic. The choices of shopping are not as extensive as other capital city airports in Asia. Many options to shop and dine are in place. Low-cost airlines when arriving, tend to disembark away from the terminal building. Disembarking passengers are ferried by bus to the terminal building. Departure is normally via air bridge. Taxi ranks and bus services are available to get you to the city.

Skybridge Cable Car, Langkawi Malaysia

Siem Reap International Airport

In keeping with the architecture in Cambodia and Siem Reap, the airport terminal in Siem Reap resembles a wooden carved temple, in fact, an incredibly beautiful building. Inside is very spacious and functional. A few shops are available after you clear customs, but most people are eager to start their holiday and do not tarry. On arrival, if you do not have a prearranged e-visa, you enter the customs area where people will fill out their forms and line up behind the official barriers, up to a dozen uniformed customs officers will check your passport details and approve your visa. It is amazing to watch the process. Firstly, you will give your passport forms and entry fee to the first officer, it will then be passed on to the second and then each one will pass your documents in turn to the next in line. Each official will do something, inspect or stamp. Your passport travels to the end of the line, your names are called and then you can leave with your visa. It passes the time while you are waiting for your visa to be processed. Soon a new international airport will commence operation after construction is completed. It is planned to be operational in 2023. The current location is a short trip from the city centre, the new location will be a fifty-minute commute.

Of course, there are many other airports in Southeast Asia, but I just included a few of the most popular ones and hope that this will assist.

LANGUAGE

The following are essential phrases and words to assist, during your travels to Asia. English is of course widely spoken in the tourist industry, and you will have no problems communicating in markets, hotels, cafes, and bars. As a sign of respect, it is always nice to be able to greet people in the local language, and to be able to ask the price. It shows good manners to say, *thank you, please,* or *excuse me,* when appropriate. The following phrases are phonetically spelt out to assist. I have tried to include common phrases, if in doubt revert to English, it will not be a problem. French is also widely spoken in Vietnam and Cambodia.

Vietnamese

Hello	Sin Chow
Thank you	Cam On
Goodbye	Tam Biet.
Excuse me/Sorry	Sin Loy
How Much?	Baow Nyee
Too Expensive	Mack Wa
Yes	Yang Da
No	Khong
Can I have the bill?	Din Ting
Please	Laam Ern

Thai

Hello	Saw Wat Dee Ka (female) Krab (male)
Thank you	Korn Kun
Goodbye	Lah Gorn
Excuse me/Sorry	Kor a Pai
How Much?	Tow Rai
Too Expensive	Phaeng Pai
Yes	Chai
No	Mai
Can I have the bill?	Kor Bin Noy
Please	Kor

Malay

Hello	Helo
Thank you	Terima Kasih
Goodbye	Selamat Tin gal
Excuse me/Sorry	Maaf
How Much?	Berapa Harganya

Too Expensive	Sangat Mahal
Yes	Yaa
No	Tidak
Can I have the bill?	Tolong Bawa Bil
Please	Silakan

Kumer (**Cambodia**)

Hello	Johm Riab Sua
Thank you	Aw Kohn
Goodbye	Lia Suhn Hao-y
Excuse me/Sorry	Sohm Toh
How Much?	Nih T-lay Pohnmaan
Too Expensive	T'Lay
Yes	Baat (male) Jaa (female)
No	Te
Can I have the bill?	Sohm Kuht Lui
Please	Sohm

Boat traffic jam on Ha Long Bay

CONCLUSION

I hope you have enjoyed reading my travel guide, we have tried to put in as many little hints and hacks to ensure that you avoid pitfalls along the way, I am sure you will enjoy your holiday in Asia. I have strived to save you from making the mistakes I made. There is so much more to know, so much more to explore and experience. We are planning to produce travel-help podcasts and develop our travel groups soon.

All group trips will include internal inside Asia airfares, accommodation, tours, hotel and airport transfers, visas (if required), many meals on organised tours and breakfast in hotel accommodation. We can, of course, assist with your booking flights from your home to Asia.

We can also cater for those wishing to travel into the region solo. Feel free to contact us as we have a service to walk you through planning and booking your trip with our assistance. If you live close, we may be able to develop your trip in person.

Thank you for reading my book. This tome differs from many other travel books. We do not recommend individual airline companies or hotels in particular locations. We take no payments or privileges from businesses looking for recommendations. We have, while writing named several places and airlines as examples. When we develop tours, we will be talking to these companies to endeavour to get the best prices and pass on these savings.

While reading this book I hope you have filed many *how-to* hints to ensure your holiday is a success. Much information is available on where to go and what to see when you arrive, but very little is around to pass on the skills on how to travel. Seasoned travellers will tell you that they picked up their travel nous after many trips and that is, of course, true, but why should you have to endure before getting the best results.

Feel free to give me any feedback. I would also love to hear from anyone who has further tips to enhance a trip to the region. Always keen to develop a second edition with new advice. My webpage will have information about blogs, details regarding guided tours and assistance to self-organise a solo trip.

Contact us at
www.EziAsiaTravel.com
EziAsiaTravel@gmail.com.
@EziAsiaTravel

Riding through Georgetown in a tri-shaw with Aziz my driver.

Lady Buddha Temple, Danang Vietnam

Japanese Bridge Hoi An Vietnam

Healthy street food in Ho Chi Min City

Angkor Wat, steep climb and decent, watch your step on the way down.

Riverside café, Hoi An Vietnam

Apsara Dancer in Cambodia

ACKNOWLEDGEMENTS

Many have contributed to the completion of this book. Some have been travel partners on my adventures, others have been fellow travellers meet along the way. Advice, both professional and personal has been offered along with encouragement. My thanks to the hundreds of friendly smiles and valuable advice given freely from locals every day that made all my trips memorable. It is clear that I would not have such a love of travel if I had not soaked in the pride of country shown by so many persons met in each and every city. After the completion of this book, I listed the names of those I have travelled, and I was surprised at the number of people I have shared experiences. I will list these in alphabetical order later. I am often astounded when people whom I had a fleeting encounter, remember me by name a year later when I've revisited.

A special thanks to Linda Lindsey for permission to use one of her pictures in the book, this was a big help.

A number of people went above and beyond in making me feel welcome and enhanced my experiences, some were fellow travellers, others local business operators. Thank you to David and Rachael (UK), Larry and Thongbi (Palm Gardens Resort Bangsaphan, Thailand), Monday Hong (Siem Reap, Cambodia), Phuc Dinh (Hanoi), Deibby Mamahit (Singapore), Boey Lee (China).

Whilst I have travelled solo at times mainly for business, I must admit that sharing a trip with friends and family is an amazing way to travel. I would not have enjoyed my time away from home without the following over the past years: Blake, Brett, Collette, Danika, Hayley, Harry, Isaac, Levi, Nicola, Orlando, Pam, Ruth, Rhonda, Shane, Sharon, and Peter.

Lastly, a special thank you to Karen who over the last few months has been a sounding board whilst in the process of completing this book. I hope in a small way this book allows new and fellow travellers to find as much joy out of my time in Southeast Asia as I have over the years and into the future.

CPSIA information can be obtained
at www.ICGtesting.com
Printed in the USA
BVHW052238041121
620781BV00009BA/257

9 780645 201383